W9-CAP-265

Pebble

Helpers in Our Community

We Need School Bus Drivers

by Helen Frost

Consulting Editor: Gail Saunders-Smith, PhD
Consultant: Ted Finlayson-Schueler
Executive Director, Pupil Transportation Safety Institute
Syracuse, New York

Boca Raton Public Library, Boca Raton, FL

Capstone
press

Mankato, Minnesota

Pebble Books are published by Capstone Press
151 Good Counsel Drive, P.O. Box 669, Mankato, Minnesota 56002
www.capstonepress.com

1 2 3 4 5 6 09 08 07 06 05 04

Library of Congress Cataloging-in-Publication Data
Frost, Helen, 1949–
    We need school bus drivers / by Helen Frost.
    p. cm.—(Helpers in our community)
    Includes bibliographical references and index.
    ISBN-13: 978-0-7368-2577-1 (hardcover)
    ISBN-10: 0-7368-2577-0 (hardcover)
    1. School buses—Juvenile literature. 2. Bus drivers—Juvenile literature.
[1. School buses. 2. Bus drivers.] I. Title. II. Series.
LB2864.F76 2005
371.8′72—dc22   2003024243

Summary: Simple text and photographs describe the role of school bus drivers.

Note to Parents and Teachers

The Helpers in Our Community series supports national social studies standards related to community helpers and their roles. This book describes and illustrates school bus drivers. The photographs support early readers in understanding the text. The repetition of words and phrases helps early readers learn new words. This book also introduces early readers to subject-specific vocabulary words, which are defined in the Glossary. Early readers may need assistance to read some words and to use the Table of Contents, Glossary, Read More, Internet Sites, and Index/Word List sections of the book.

Table of Contents

School Bus Drivers

School bus drivers
drive children to
and from school.

School bus drivers
make sure buses
are safe and clean.

School bus drivers
pick up children
at school bus stops.

School bus drivers put
out a stop sign. They
turn on flashing lights.
Then cars stop to let
children cross the street.

Helping Children

School bus drivers open bus doors. Children get on the buses.

14

Some children need help getting on buses. School bus drivers help them.

At School

School bus drivers stop at schools. They make sure children get off the buses safely.

School bus drivers
pick up children after
school. They drive children
back to their bus stops.

School bus drivers
help keep children safe.

Glossary

clean—not dirty or messy

safe—not in danger of being harmed

school bus—a large vehicle that brings students to and from school; school buses are usually yellow.

school bus stop—a place where children wait for school buses to come and pick them up; school buses also drop off children at school bus stops.

stop sign—a red sign that warns drivers to stop; a school bus has a stop sign on the side of the bus.

Read More

Gorman, Jacqueline Laks. *Bus Driver.* People in My Community. Milwaukee: Weekly Reader Early Learning Library, 2002.

Owen, Ann. *Taking You Places: A Book about Bus Drivers.* Community Workers. Minneapolis: Picture Window Books, 2004.

Internet Sites

FactHound offers a safe, fun way to find Internet sites related to this book. All of the sites on FactHound have been researched by our staff.

Here's how:

1. Visit *www.facthound.com*
2. Type in this special code **0736825770** for age-appropriate sites. Or enter a search word related to this book for a more general search.
3. Click on the **Fetch It** button.

FactHound will fetch the best sites for you!

Index/Word List

bus stops, 9, 19
cars, 11
clean, 7
cross, 11
doors, 13
drive, 5, 19
help, 15, 21

lights, 11
open, 13
pick up, 9, 19
safe, 7, 17, 21
stop, 11, 17
stop sign, 11
street, 11

Word Count: 112
Early-Intervention Level: 11

Editorial Credits

Mari C. Schuh, editor; Abby Bradford, Bradford Design Inc., cover designer; Enoch Peterson, book designer; Wanda Winch, photo researcher; Karen Hieb, product planning editor

Photo Credits

AP/Kim D. Johnson, 6
Corbis/Julie Habel, 4; LWA-Dann Tardif, 20
EyeWire Images, 1
Folio Inc./Tom McCarthy Photos, 16
Photodisc Inc., 8
Photri-Microstock/Jeff Greenberg, 14; Mark Gibson, 12
Unicorn Stock Photos/Jeff Greenberg, 10; M. Siluk, 18
West Hawaii Today/Michael Darden, cover

The author thanks the children's library staff at the Allen County Public Library, Fort Wayne, Indiana, for research assistance.

24